The Museum

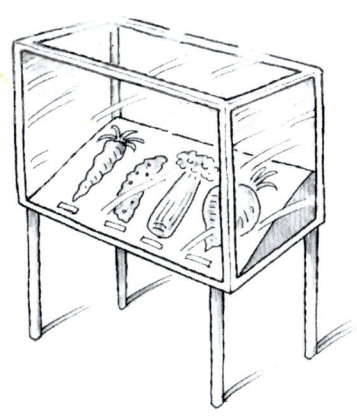

Contents

The Food Museum	4
A Meal to Remember	12
The Camping Trip	21
Vocabulary	30
Story Questions	32

Titles in the Runway series

Level 4
The Street
The Wish
The Magic Shop
The Ghost House

Level 5
Trapped
The Rumour
The Food Museum
Escape from the City

Level 6
The Good Student
Virtual Teacher
Football Smash
The Empty House

Badger Publishing Limited
15 Wedgwood Gate, Pin Green Industrial Estate,
Stevenage, Hertfordshire SG1 4SU
Telephone: 01438 356907. Fax: 01438 747015
www.badger-publishing.co.uk
enquiries@badger-publishing.co.uk

The Food Museum ISBN 978 1 84691 372 3

Text © Jillian Powell, Alison Hawes 2008
Complete work © Badger Publishing Limited 2008

All rights reserved. No part of this publication may be reproduced, stored in any form or by any means mechanical, electronic, recording or otherwise without the prior permission of the publisher.

The right of Jillian Powell and Alison Hawes to be identified as the authors of this Work has been asserted by them in accordance with the Copyright, Designs and Patents Act 1988.

Publisher: David Jamieson
Commissioning Editor: Carrie Lewis
Design: Fiona Grant
Illustration: Robin Lawrie, Aleksandar Sotirovski, Enzo Troiano

The Food Museum

Written by Jillian Powell
Illustrated by Robin Lawrie

The school children were at the food museum.

The first room was about fruit and vegetables.

The next room was about meat and fish.

They learned about bacon, beef, chicken and seafoods.

They saw an old film about milking cows.

The next room was about tools for eating.

They learned how people used knives, forks and spoons to eat.

Next, they saw pictures of supermarkets and restaurants.

They learned that people once had to shop for food.

They each had to draw one kind of food.

It was time for a break.

They all went outside to get chips.

The chips went into their arms.

They gave them energy, just as food once did, in the past.

A Meal to Remember

Written by Alison Hawes
Illustrated by Aleksander Sotirovski

It was Sam's birthday.
Her dad took her to a top restaurant.

Sam and her dad looked at the big menu.

Sam ordered a pasta dish.
Her dad ordered a fish dish.

The waiter brought their food.

It was delicious.

Then the waiter brought a birthday cake.
Everyone sang, "Happy Birthday."

Dad had to go home to get his credit card. Sam had to wait in the restaurant.

Everyone was looking at her.

Dad came back.
He was very red.

He couldn't find his credit card.
The waiter was very angry.

Sam and her dad had to do the washing up.

Dad was very sorry.
But Sam was *very* angry!

The Camping Trip

Written by Alison Hawes
Illustrated by Enzo Troiano

Jamie and Mark wanted to go camping.
Jamie packed the tent and sleeping bags.
Mark packed the plates and tins of food.

They walked past the houses.
They walked past the shops.
They walked and walked until they came to trees and fields.

Jamie unpacked the tent and sleeping bags.
Mark unpacked the plates and tins of food.

"I'll put up the tent," said Jamie.

"I'll cook some food," said Mark.

But Mark couldn't find the tin opener.
There were mugs and knives and forks – but no tin opener!

Jamie was very hungry and very cross.
Mark tried to open the tins with a knife.
But it was no good.

Then Mark had an idea.
He phoned for help.
"Did you phone your mum?" asked Jamie.

"No," said Mark. "I phoned for a pizza!"

Vocabulary

The Food Museum

food
museum
fruit
vegetables
carrots
underground
meat
fish
bacon
beef
chicken
seafood

animals
milking
cows
drink
knives
forks
spoons
supermarkets
restaurants
burger
chips
energy

A Meal to Remember

restaurant
menu
ordered
food
pasta
dish
fish
waiter

delicious
bill

The Camping Trip

plates
tent
tins
sleeping bags
packed/unpacked
food
cook
tin opener
mugs
knives
forks
pizza

Story questions

The Food Museum

Do carrots grow on trees?
What do the children find out about milk?
Is this story in our time?

A Meal to Remember

Do Sam and her Dad order the same dish?
Whose birthday was it?
Was Sam right to be angry?

The Camping Trip

What did Jamie pack for the camping trip?
Why did Jamie get cross?
Was calling for a pizza a good idea?